ALLIGATORS AND CROCODILES

by **HERBERT S. ZIM**

Copy 1

Illustrated by

James Gordon Irving

WILLIAM MORROW & COMPANY
New York   1952

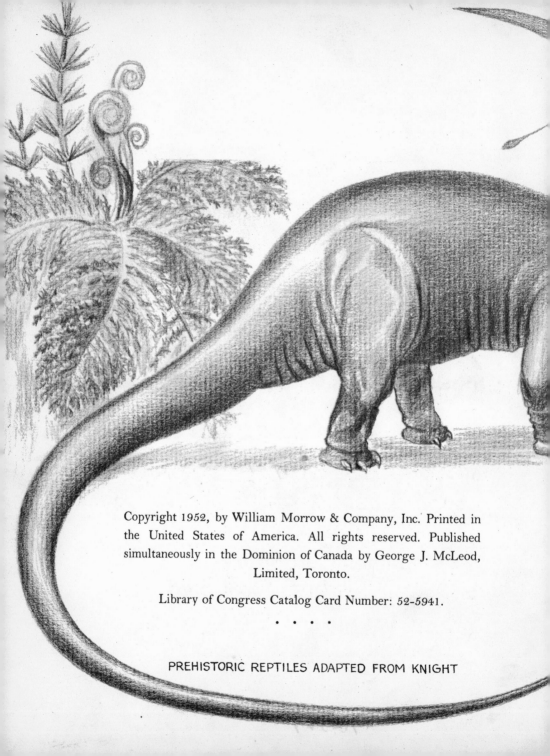

Library of Congress Catalog Card Number: 52-5941.

. . . .

PREHISTORIC REPTILES ADAPTED FROM KNIGHT

About one hundred and twenty
million years ago reptiles were
the most important animals on
earth. The largest ones, dinosaurs,
plodded through the great lush
swamps. Other reptiles swam the
seas. Still others roamed the
deserts, and some even flew

3

through the air. About seventy million years ago these giant reptiles died off. Only four groups of reptiles live today—lizards, snakes, turtles, and alligators. The last group is the one that is most like the giant reptiles of the past.

TURTLES

LIZARDS

SNAKES

ALLIGATORS AND CROCODILES

REPTILES OF TODAY

By studying fossil bones buried
in ancient rocks, scientists learn
what the great reptiles were like.
Fossils prove that certain kinds
of alligators and crocodiles were
living during the Age of Reptiles.
Bones also show that alligators
and crocodiles today are very
much like those of long ago.

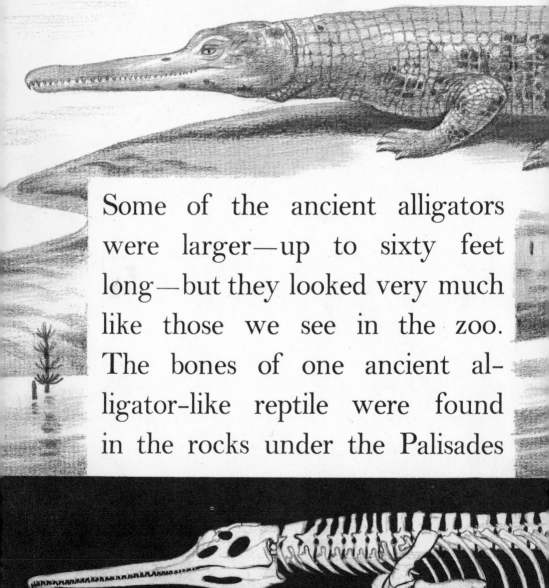

Some of the ancient alligators were larger—up to sixty feet long—but they looked very much like those we see in the zoo. The bones of one ancient alligator-like reptile were found in the rocks under the Palisades

PHYTOSAUR AS IT MAY
HAVE APPEARED ALIVE

near New York City. Bones of another were discovered in the rocks of the famous Petrified Forest of Arizona. Fossil bones of alligators and their kin have been found in other places where no alligators live today.

PHYTOSAUR SKELETON RESTORED
(ADAPTED FROM McGREGOR)

About twenty kinds of alligators and similar reptiles live
in the warmer parts of the world:
in Asia, Africa, Australia, and
both Americas. They live in

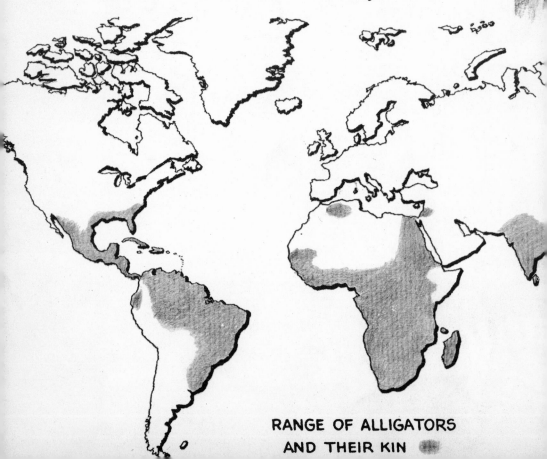

**RANGE OF ALLIGATORS
AND THEIR KIN**

rivers, swamps, lagoons, bays, and in fresh and salt marshes. Alligators and crocodiles are water reptiles, though they like to lie in the sun on river banks. If they are disturbed, they rush headlong back to the water, where they feel safer and more at home.

ALLIGATOR'S FEET

FRONT FOOT   BACK FOOT

From head to toe these reptiles are fitted for water life. Their toes (five on the front feet, four on the back) are webbed. They use their webbed feet to paddle slowly and keep balanced in

1

ALLIGATOR SWIMMING

ALLIGATOR PADDLING SLOWLY

the water. An alligator swims with its strong, powerful tail and, when chased, it can swim faster than two men can paddle a canoe.

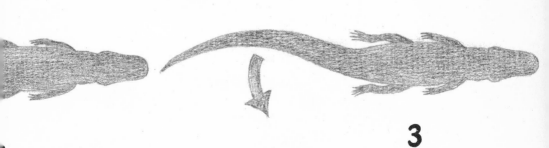

3

TAIL MOVES FROM SIDE TO SIDE

The alligator's long head is well fitted for life in the water. A flap of skin at the back of the mouth can close off the throat. The two nostrils, far forward on its head, connect to the back of its mouth, *behind* the flap. Because of this, the alligator can breathe when only the tip of its nose is out of water. Flaps of

THROAT

TONGUE

↓NOSTR

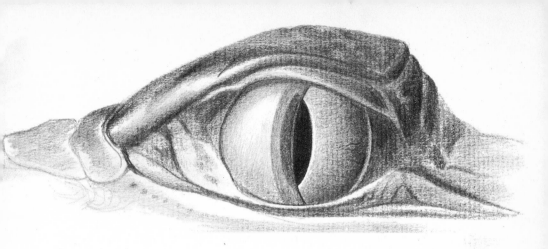

skin keep water out of the ear openings of an alligator. A thin colorless tissue moves back and forth to cover its eyes so it can see better under water. Its tough scaly hide is waterproof. An alligator can lie under water with only its eyes and nostrils out, waiting without a movement till a duck, fish, or other animal

comes close. Then, with a sudden plunge and snap, the alligator swallows its dinner.

Alligators and crocodiles are not very fussy about food. They live entirely on flesh and eat almost any animal that comes near their snapping jaws. We hear of dogs, pigs, mules, deer,

CRAB

SHRIMP   KILLIFISHES

and other large animals being killed and eaten by alligators, but this is unusual nowadays. Scientists who studied wild alligators found that about three quarters of their food consisted of small water animals like crayfish, shrimp, crabs, water beetles, and

GAR

MENHADEN

DUCKS

CRAYFISH

OADS AND FROGS

TURTLES

FOOD OF ALLIGATORS

RABBITS

YOUNG ALLIGATORS

SMALL PIGS

COOTS

SNAKES

MUSKRATS

MORE FOOD OF ALLIGATORS

other insects. More of these smaller animals are eaten by young alligators. About a quarter of the alligator's food consists of fish, ducks and other water birds, turtles, snakes, muskrats, rabbits, and, every now and then, another alligator or a large animal.

Do alligators eat people? In the case of the American alligator, the answer is "never" or "hardly ever." Stories of alligators attacking people are hard to prove. Perhaps a century ago, when alligators were larger and more common, this may have happened more often. Many reports prove that alligators fear people. Men have often bathed in waters where alligators live,

without being bothered. The crocodiles of Africa, Malaya, and the East Indies are another story. Some have long been known as dangerous killers.

If alligators and crocodiles sometimes attack people, the reverse is more often true. People have killed these animals till they are now far less common than in the past. From 1800 to 1900 about three million alligators were killed in Florida alone. For a long time alligator skins, worth a half

million dollars or more, were sold each year. Large alligators were killed for sport or for their skins. Young ones were captured and sold as souvenirs. Swamps were drained and coastal marshes were often replaced by farms and growing cities. The homes of the alligators were destroyed.

Finally, after nine out of every ten alligators had been killed, laws were passed to protect them.

The hunting season has been limited, and there are places, particularly the breeding grounds, where alligators cannot be hunted at all. Everglades National Park in Florida is one of these.

WILDLIFE REFUGE

For some time, visitors to Florida and other southern states shipped baby alligators home for pets. But young alligators do not make good pets. They are difficult to feed and care for. They need a place that is warmer than the average house. If they are cold they do not eat, and finally die. Now it is against the law to ship these young alligators.

Alligators do not have young till they are five or six years old. The males and females mate during the spring and the female usually lays her eggs in June, though some may lay earlier or later. Each female builds a nest on the ground above the water level. She drags leaves and branches, cattails, rushes, grass, and mud, and makes a rough mound, five to eight feet across and about three feet high. She scoops out a rough hole on top and lays her eggs in it. A young female lays fewer eggs than an

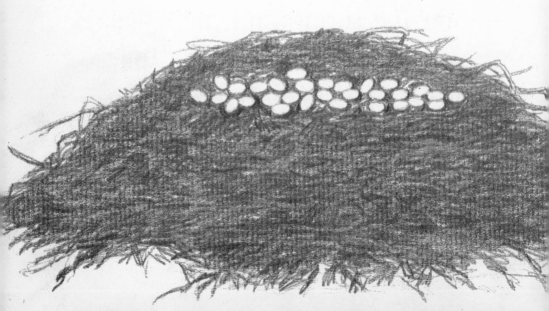

INSIDE AN ALLIGATOR'S NEST

HEN

BULL SNAKE

ALLIGATOR

SOME DIFFERENT EGGS

older one does. In general, a female lays from twenty to sixty white, hard-shelled eggs, each as big as a large hen's egg. The eggs are covered with rotted leaves, grass, pieces of plants, and mud. The mother stays near them all the time.

If the nest stays moist, the heat of the sun and the heat of the rotting plants will hatch the eggs in eight or nine weeks. If the weather is too dry or if the nest is flooded, the eggs may not hatch at all. Skunks, raccoons, and other egg eaters sometimes raid the nest. These raids would be more common if the mother alligator were not on guard. Finally the eggs hatch.

EGG   **ALLIGATOR EMBRYO**

The mother, who is always near, tears the nest apart to let her young escape. The young alligators scamper for the water. Their mother leads them off to a safe place, where they stay with her till the following spring.

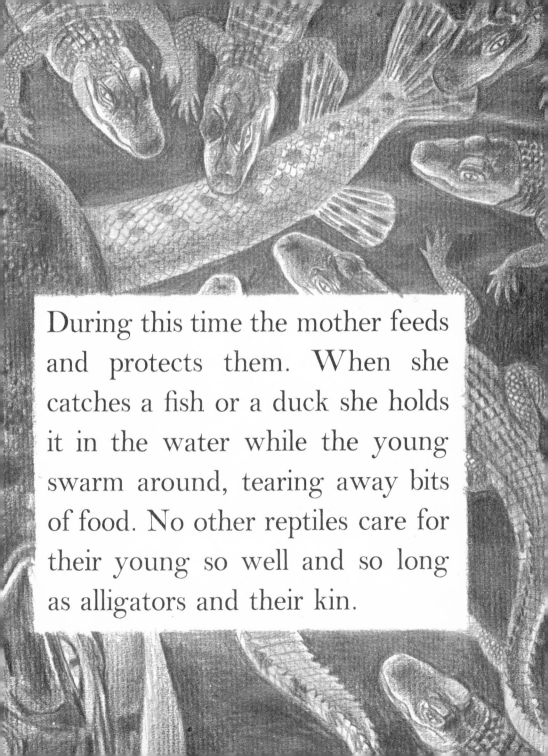

During this time the mother feeds and protects them. When she catches a fish or a duck she holds it in the water while the young swarm around, tearing away bits of food. No other reptiles care for their young so well and so long as alligators and their kin.

When they hatch, the yellow-banded black alligators are about nine inches long and weigh less than two ounces. In a year they are about two feet long and weigh nine or ten ounces. They continue to grow rapidly, and when five years old are over five feet long, and weigh thirty to forty pounds. If they live till they are ten, alligators may be as big as ten feet long and may weigh several hundred pounds.

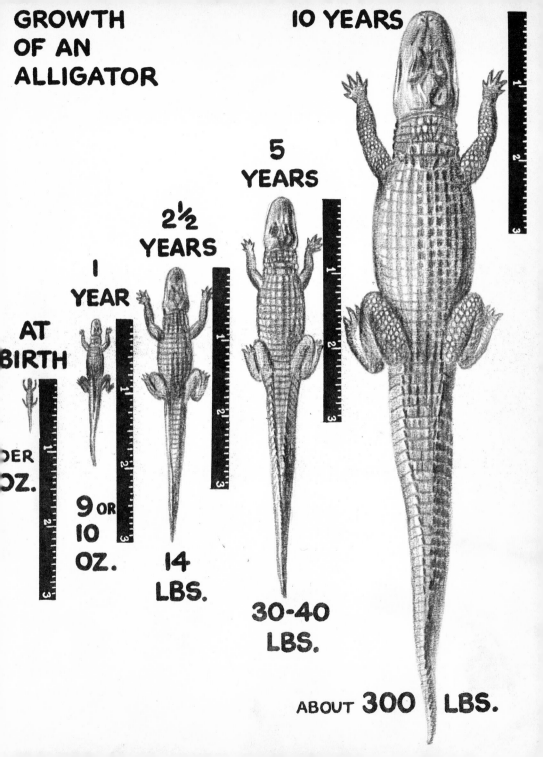

GROWTH
OF AN
ALLIGATOR

10 YEARS

5
YEARS

2½
YEARS

1
YEAR

AT
BIRTH

...DER
...OZ.

9 OR
10
OZ.

14
LBS.

30-40
LBS.

ABOUT 300 LBS.

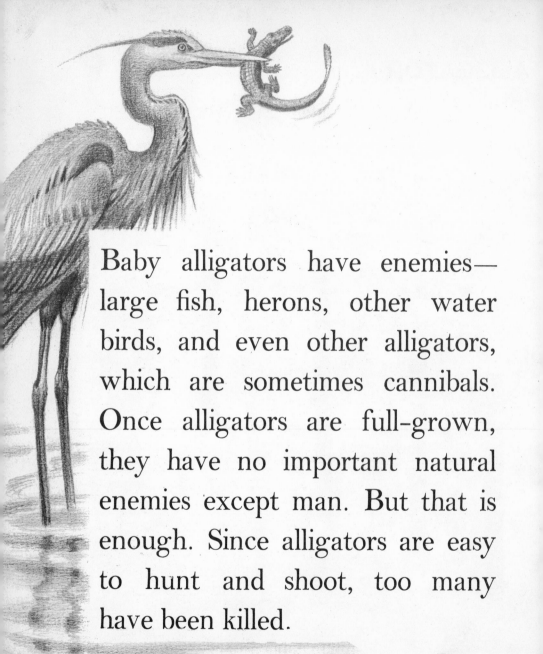

Baby alligators have enemies— large fish, herons, other water birds, and even other alligators, which are sometimes cannibals. Once alligators are full-grown, they have no important natural enemies except man. But that is enough. Since alligators are easy to hunt and shoot, too many have been killed.

The full-grown alligator prefers to lead an easy life. In a plant-choked stream or in a swamp it may tear away the plants to make a deep, open-water "gator hole." Or it may find a place where the river is deep and dig itself a den. This may be made under an overhanging bank where it can seek shelter. The

alligator may dig a long tunnel or it may find a cave with an underwater entrance. Some caves seem to end above the water level, so the alligator has a dry den. An alligator often uses the same den as long as it lives.

As the weather gets colder, the alligator becomes less and less active. It eats little or not at all. If the air is warm, the alligator may come out on dry ground to bask in the sun. If it is cold, it stays in the water or

in its den. In spring it becomes active again.

An alligator spends a good part of its time in the water, lying perfectly still with only eyes and nostrils above the

surface. Sometimes it swims or pushes its way through shallow water in search of food. Like all other reptiles, the alligator is cold-blooded. This means that its body is about as warm as the air or water around it. The alligator seems to prefer a temperature of 90 to 95 degrees.

WARM- AND COLD-BLOODED ANIMALS :

WHEN THE AIR IS 70° THE
TEMPERATURE OF THESE
WARM-BLOODED ANIMALS IS
98.6°
MAN

WHEN THE AIR IS 70° TH
TEMPERATURE OF ALL TH
COLD-BLOODED ANIMALS IS
70°

BULLFROG

DOG
100.5°

GREEN
SNAKE

MARBLED SALAMANDER

106°
CHICKEN

BOX TURTLE

RABBIT ## 102°

ALLIGATOR

While many alligators live in the same area, each claims and keeps a piece of land around its den or nest and protects it from invaders. Here the alligator lives and hunts. When one alligator pulls a large animal like a deer or pig under water, another may come over to grab the victim and help tear it to pieces.

The alligator uses its pointed teeth for grasping and holding. It does not chew like a dog or a cow, but will crush a small animal's bones and swallow it

YOU HAVE SEVERAL KINDS OF TEETH

INCISOR	CANINE	PREMOLARS AND MOLARS

FOR CUTTING	FOR TEARING	FOR GRINDING

ALLIGATORS HAVE ONLY ONE KIND OF TEET
SOME ARE LARGER THAN OTHERS

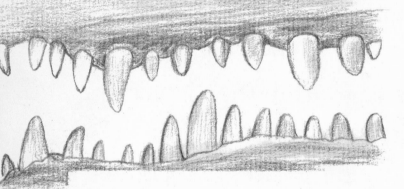

CROWN

ROOT

whole. Each powerful jaw has
seventeen to twenty teeth, all
about the same shape. Teeth fall
out every now and then when

ALLIGATOR TOOTH

NEW TOOTH GROWING IN

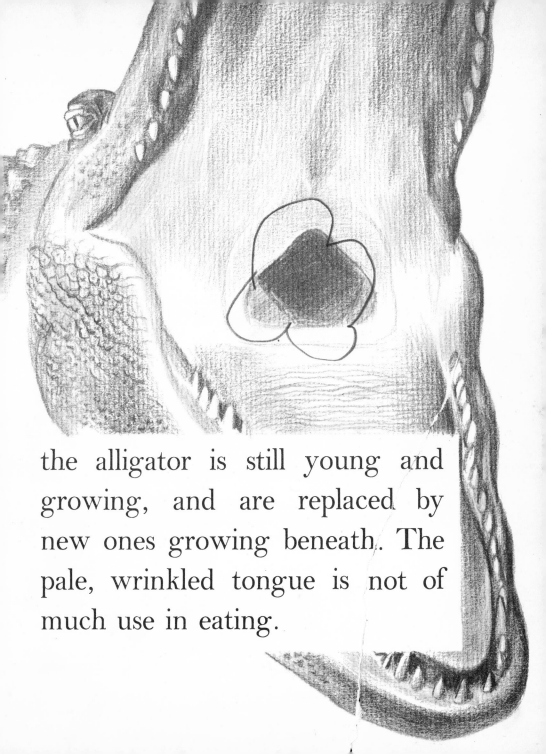

the alligator is still young and growing, and are replaced by new ones growing beneath. The pale, wrinkled tongue is not of much use in eating.

For a stiff-necked, armor-plated animal, the alligator is very agile. It can move fast on land and even faster in the water. Its heavy, powerful tail is used for swimming and fighting. With its tail, a large alligator can deal a blow that will break a man's leg. The alligator cannot turn its head very much, but can curve

its body and snap at either side. An alligator over five feet long can be very dangerous.

The alligator is one of the few reptiles with a voice. Even the very young can bark. Older ones roar and bellow, and when the huge old alligators were still alive, it is said that they sounded like foghorns. The roaring of alligators is most often heard on spring nights when the males are

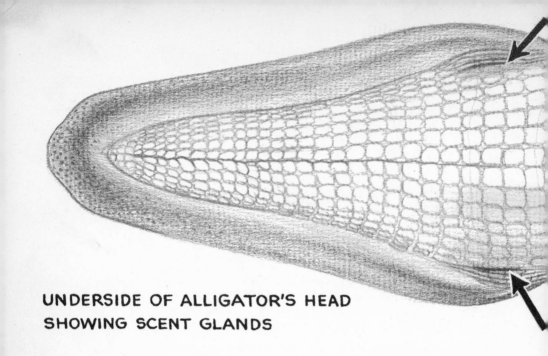

**UNDERSIDE OF ALLIGATOR'S HEAD
SHOWING SCENT GLANDS**

getting ready to mate. As they roar, two glands under their jaws open and give out a musky scent which fills the swamp air and may attract the females. At this time the males become fiercer and fight with one another.

When the mating season is over, the females turn to building or rebuilding their nests. After laying their eggs, they live and feed nearby. The males go back to their own easy life in the warm summer sun.

The name *alligator* seems to be nothing more than the English way of saying the Spanish name of the animal: *el lagarto*. The Spaniards, who discovered and explored the warmer parts of America, were the first Europeans to see these huge reptiles. Like most early explorers, they added

fanciful details to the reports they took back home. Stories of huge man-eating monsters with bullet-proof skins were told and retold. When people finally began to study alligators seriously, it was hard to tell if the old stories about their size, age, and habits were really true. The experts think the largest alligator ever measured was slightly more than nineteen feet in length. From end to end he was a little more than three times the height of a tall man. An alligator over ten feet long is rare today.

LARGEST KNOWN ALLIGATOR

It was once believed that large alligators were very old—perhaps a century old or more. Now we know that alligators grow about a foot a year when young, so large size does not have to mean great age. At twenty, a wild alligator is fairly old. However, in zoos, where food is plentiful and conditions are good, alligators have lived as long as forty years.

OLD MOSE
AMERICAN ALLIGATOR
Alligator mississippi
SOUTH EASTERN
UNITED STA

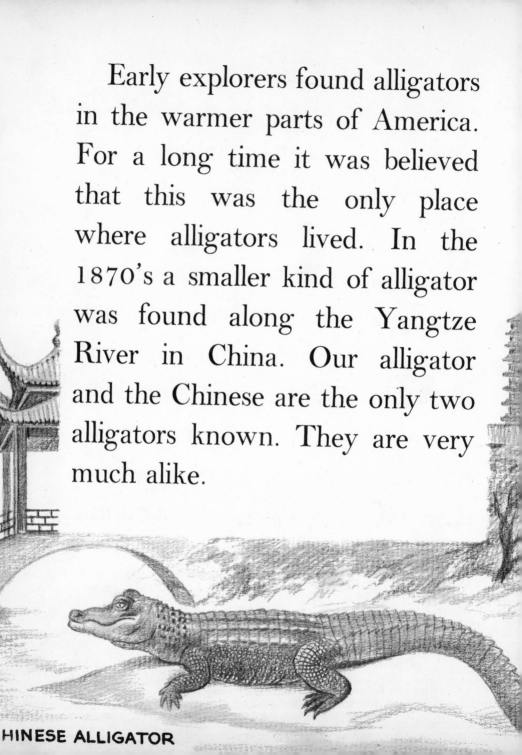

Early explorers found alligators in the warmer parts of America. For a long time it was believed that this was the only place where alligators lived. In the 1870's a smaller kind of alligator was found along the Yangtze River in China. Our alligator and the Chinese are the only two alligators known. They are very much alike.

CHINESE ALLIGATOR

AMERICAN CROCODILE

Crocodiles, however, have long been known in Africa, Asia, and Australia. But it was not till 1875 that a crocodile was discovered in southern Florida. The Florida crocodile prefers warmer water than alligators do. In this country the crocodile has never been very common, nor has it spread very far. Alligators, as the map shows,

10341

live all along the south Atlantic and Gulf coasts. In this country crocodiles are found only in southern Florida.

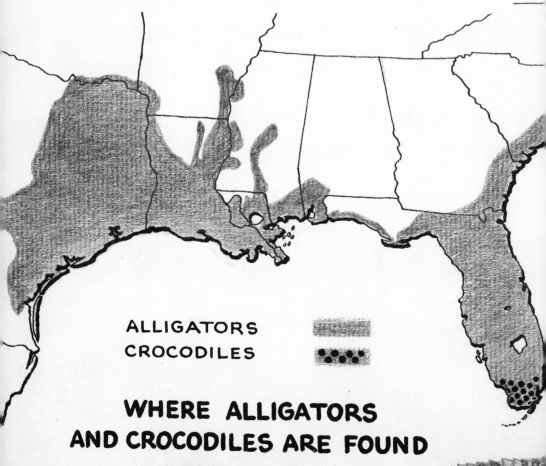

ALLIGATORS
CROCODILES

WHERE ALLIGATORS AND CROCODILES ARE FOUND

Alligators and crocodiles are closely related, but a few clear differences make it easy for anyone to tell one from the other. The Florida crocodile is smaller, thinner, and more agile than the alligator. It is blackish in color, while the alligator is olive or

CROCODILE

ALLIGATOR

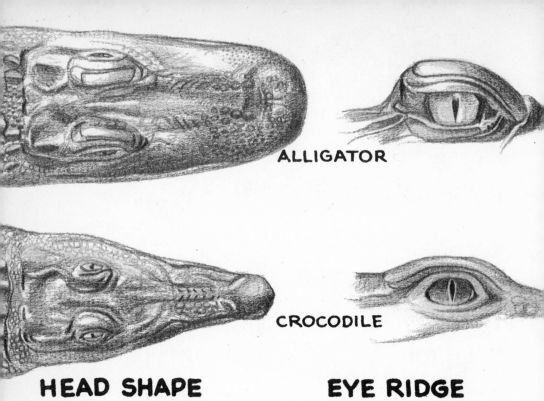

ALLIGATOR

CROCODILE

HEAD SHAPE   **EYE RIDGE**

gray. The principal differences
are in the head. The crocodile's
is more narrow and pointed. The
eyes stick out farther and the ear
openings are easier to see. The

ALLIGATOR

CROCODILE

crocodile has fewer teeth, but
they are longer and sharper than
the alligator's. Two teeth in the
lower jaw stick up, bulldog
fashion. Crocodiles prefer salt

55

swamps and bays, while alligators like fresh water better. Men who have hunted both animals say crocodiles are more wary and harder to find. They are quicker, meaner, and more vicious when captured.

There are ten kinds of crocodiles, which differ from one another in size and markings, and live in various places. The crocodile found in Florida also lives in Central and South America. Another kind lives along the warm coasts of Central America. Cuba has a kind all its own. Another variety lives in the Orinoco River in Venezuela. The largest crocodiles are the Nile crocodile, found in many African rivers and lakes, and the saltwater crocodile of the Malay region of Asia and the East Indies. These two greatly feared, man-eating crocodiles grow over twenty feet long. The salt-water crocodile lives along the shores, in salt swamps, and at the mouths of rivers, but it has sometimes been found at sea, far from land. The crocodile of the Nile was held sacred by the ancient Egyptians. In tombs and temples, mummies of thousands of these reptiles have been found.

Another group of large reptiles, more like alligators than crocodiles, lives in the waters of Central America and tropical South America. These are the caimans. Five different kinds are found, some growing as long as

YOUNG CROCODILE
MUMMY WITH
LINEN WRAPPINGS

twenty feet, if local reports are true. Most of the caimans have narrower snouts than alligators. The teeth in their upper and lower jaws fit as those of alligators do. Though they are common along the Amazon and other rivers, they are not considered dangerous to man.

The gavials, or garials, of Asia are the only other group related to alligators and crocodiles. One kind lives along the Ganges and other rivers in India, another in

SKULLS

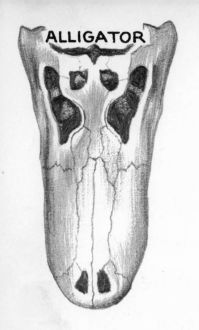

ALLIGATOR

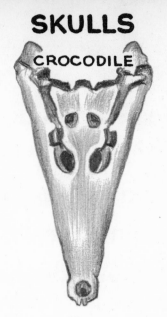

CROCODILE

GAVIAL

Borneo and Sumatra. The gavials, too, may grow as long as twenty feet. They are reported to be timid and not dangerous to man. The food of the gavial is largely fish. Its very long, thin, pointed snout, with many sharp teeth, is best fitted for grasping fish.

Alligators, crocodiles, and their kin are all we have left of the ancient giant reptiles that once ruled the earth. Even if they had no other value, they would be interesting as living fossils, reminders of the days when the earth was younger.

Grateful recognition is given to
Dr. William H. Stickel,
United States Fish and Wildlife Service,
for reading and criticizing the manuscript
and to
Dr. Hobart Smith,
University of Illinois,
for checking the illustrations.